© 2022, Kiera Webster
Production and publishing:
BoD - Books on Demand, Norderstedt
ISBN: 9783756844272

I remember the way the world stood still when I heard Mom say it. Three words, said all too calmly, not even to me; just something I overheard.

It was March, maybe an hour or two after I'd come home from school. Fourth grade, it was cloudy that day, but everything was fine. I was enjoying some plain Costco ruffle chips on the couch, scribbling around on one of those old magnetic drawing boards without a care in the world. The doorbell rang.

I guess I get why Mom was so… okay, so nonchalant about it. It must've been like going home to her. Her footsteps grew louder as she rounded the cornered staircase, one of her daycare kids in tow. She opened the door and greeted the kid's dad, made some small talk about his kid's day, the usual. I wasn't paying much attention, she spoke to all of her kid's parents like this, so I just kept crunching.

He asked a question. A question that I, in that second, didn't understand why he'd ask. My crunching stopped prematurely, my mouth still full of half-chewed chips, I couldn't risk the answer being obstructed by the sound of me absolutely obliterating my favourite salty snack.

"Yup, it's official."

It took a second to process, and when it did, it hit me like a brick. A lot of bricks, actually. Like a whole house amount of bricks. The man said some sort of congratulations, I have no idea for what. My entire life was just flipped upside down, inside out, torn apart, reglued shoddily by a kindergartener with a hot glue gun and then thrown into a lake in not even a full sentence, but yeah, sure, congrats.

Man, I thought the initial shock would kill me. The future, as I could foresee it, disappeared right in front of me. In that moment, I dissolved into a tiny, ten-year-old ball of pure distress... but what I didn't know then, was that the worst was yet to come.

1

"It's not the end of the world, Cameron, just... look at it differently. Like a new chapter", Mom suggested, frustrated by my indignance.

We were sitting together at the dinner table, not for food, but to discuss the "situation", if you will. Mom had come prepared with a piece of paper and a sharpie, her brilliant idea to get me on board consisted of a pro and con list.

"You've shut down every pro we mentioned", Dad said, "you won't be happy if you don't look at the positives at all."

"Because there are no positives", I argued.

"Good lord, Cameron, there *are* positives. Read the list!", Dad growled, becoming even more frustrated with my attitude than he already was.

"New village to explore", Mom began listing.

"Already seen it", I countered.

Mom sighed. "Okay, fine, new landscape."

"I don't like the mountains, they're hard to walk up."

She huffed. "New friends, isn't that cool? Meeting new people!"

"What about my old friends?", I provoked, "oh, and new friends *how?* I can't speak German, remember?"

"Okay, another pro, you'll learn a new language. That's a privilege *and* a benefit!"

"And what if I forget English?"

"What? You won't", Mom answered, confused. Fair. I didn't make any good points, I just wanted to argue. "I didn't forget German when I moved here twenty years ago, and you'll still be speaking English at home. Speaking languages is like riding a bike."

"My stuff?"

"That's enough, Cameron, you're being ridiculous now", Dad barked. "We're not going to stay here just because *you* want to. You'll thank us when you're older."

Mom closed her sharpie and dad shot me a stern look, making it obvious that there was nothing else left to say. It's true that there was nothing I could do, and I already knew that, but somehow, I just couldn't quite wrap my head around the rest of it yet. Like, that it's actually going to *happen*, that I'm actually moving. And it's not even really about the moving itself... because I could handle moving cities, or even provinces, if I have to. It's about the fact that I'm suddenly moving *four thousand miles* across the Atlantic Ocean, to a country I've been to twice, just *because*.

Thing is, this is home. Even if I haven't always lived here, it's all I know. We moved here from a suburb of Toronto when I was four. My parents were fed up with living in a cramped townhouse in the big city and wanted something quieter, not just for them, but for me, too. Dad ended up finding a job here, in a small city of about eighty-thousand people. It was quaint, calm, and safe. Perfect for us.

I barely remember moving the first time. The move was between summer and the start of junior kindergarten, meaning even if we hadn't left Toronto, I would've had to change schools anyway, which might've made things easier to digest… that or I just didn't care because I was so young. Either way, it didn't bother me like it does this time.

"Cameron", Mom called out to me after a few hours of silence, "are you ready for Cubs?"

"Aw, shoot", I thought. I'd been sulking in my room since the discussion earlier and totally forgot about tonight. "Uh, yeah… I just need to put on my shirt first", I called back, hastily grabbing my uniform from my closet.

The uniform was simple, a pair of jeans, a grey shirt we're given that we sew all our badges on to, and the classic neckerchief. The old uniform was nicer, a tan button down with a sash and everything, but I admit the new one is more comfortable. Our neckerchief is half green, half red, and honestly kind of ugly. It's tied together with the ears at the front by a slider, and no matter what I do, the neckerchief is just… too big. Like I'm all necker, no Cub.

"Do you need some help, Cam?", Mom asked as I walked out of my bedroom, struggling with my necker as usual.

"Yes, please."

She stood behind me and began folding the neckerchief. "Tonight, Cameron", she said, only half focused on her

7

own words, "And tomorrow, at school, too. Don't tell any-one that we're leaving just yet, okay?"

She slid the slider up the two-toned ears and patted my shoulders.

"…Why?", I asked coolly.

"Because", she paused for a second, "It's none of their business."

"Oh."

I walked towards the front door and sat down on the stairs, grabbing my boots and toque. Mom followed right behind and handed me my jacket from the rack beside the front door.

"Not even Wyatt?", I asked as mom slipped her jacket on.

"No", she answered, firm in her decision.

"And not Noah, either?"

"No, Cameron. Nobody."

"But if I just stop showing up to Cubs over the summer, Wyatt will think I died."

"No, he won't. He'll think you stopped going to Cubs. You can tell him the last time we go, now get up, we'll be late."

We shouted our byes to Dad before leaving the house in silence. It was cold outside, not quite dead-of-winter nose hair freezing cold like it was a few months ago, but decently chilly. The days were beginning to lengthen a little, but spring was clearly still a ways away.

Cub meet was usually in the same spot every week, only about a five-minute walk from my house if you took the shortcut. It was a very nice, well-kept church on Sunset Boulevard, I'm sure very popular when we weren't around. We always in the basement on days like today, where it's too cold to be outside all evening.

Mom and I scraped as much snow off our boots as we could before entering the church. We took off our jackets and hung them on the coat rack by the entrance before following the trail of muck left behind by wet snow boots downstairs.

Everyone was loud, excited, running around in circles as they usually were. I took refuge on the sidelines, not really interested in talking tonight.

"Cameron! Cameron, look, I have to show you something!", someone called out from the crowd.

"Ah, hi Wyatt", I said, noticing a thin, tall-ish boy weaving his way through the hyperactive crowd.

Wyatt and I met all the way back in Beavers when we were around 5, maybe 6. We became Cubs together after graduating from Beavers, and we're supposed to graduate to Scouts together, too. At least we *were.*

Wyatt pushed his rectangle-frame glasses up on his snout. "Dude, look at this, I got it today in a trade." He excitedly pulled a trading card from our favourite video game from the pocket of his jeans and swayed it back and forth, showing off the card's holographic finish. "Can you believe it? I feel kind of bad, the kid who gave it to me didn't know how rare it is. But I *needed* this card!", he geeked.

"No way, dude", I geeked back, "what did you trade?"

"A grass element and one of my dupe cards", Wyatt stuck the card back into his pocket, "it sounds bad, but I swear the kid was happy. What about you?"

"What, what about me?"

"Like, did anything cool happen this week?", he asked.

My stomach churned thinking about earlier today. I snuck a peek at Mom, who was busy talking to one of the other Cub leaders but hesitated to say anything.

"Uhh, yeah, uh, no, no. Nothing. Just like, school."

"Oh, sucks. Oh! Hey, you know how we went rowing at Brownsea Base back in the summer?", he asked, geek mode reactivated.

"Yeah, it was really cool."

"It was, holy smokes. I know you enjoyed it too. I've been thinking of signing up when I'm old enough."

One of the things I like most about Wyatt is the way you can tell when he's really interested in something. He's usually pretty subdued, he's got these sleepy, droopy blue eyes that al- ways make him look like he's ready for a nap, but boy, do they ever light up when he's excited. I knew he enjoyed the rowing then, because his tired eyes were wide awake, glowing like a bonfire at a

Cuboree, the same way they're glowing now just talking about it.

"Don't you have to be twelve for that?", I asked. Wyatt al- ready turned eleven, but he still wouldn't be twelve until after sign-up season was over.

"You do, but then I thought, if I wait until next summer, then we can sign up together! Doesn't that sound cool?"

"Uh…", I paused.

"Okay, Cubs", Mom suddenly called out from the middle of the room, where she had set up the flags for opening. Yeah, awkward. My mom is my Cub Leader. "Everyone stand in a circle for the opening ceremony!"

"Sounds cool, Wyatt", I hesitated.

"What's wrong? Not cool?", he asked, slowly moving towards the flags.

"No, it is… But I don't know if I can."

"Aw, what? Why not? Got something else going on?"

"I'm moving", I spat, "maybe. Probably. Don't tell anyone, or my mom will flip."

Wyatt nearly tripped over himself. His lowered his volume to just barely a whisper as we inched closer to the flags. Everyone was already gathered around them but us.

"No, you're kidding", he chuckled nervously, "you're just afraid, aren't you?"

He was joking, I could hear the apprehension in his voice. He hoped I was joking, too.

"I'm serious, Wyatt."

His grin faded.

"...Really?"

"Really."

He looked down towards his feet, quiet as a mouse. We shuffled into the circle around the flags for opening ceremony, Wyatt's sleepy eyes back to their tired usual. He'd never been much of a chatterbox; but that night, you would've thought he was mute.

2

"Why?"

I shrugged my shoulders. "Mom wants to go home", I said.

"But what about you?", Wyatt asked, dragging a stick through half-melted, dirty late-winter snow, knees hiked up to his chest as we sat on the stairs to the main entrance.

Mom was still inside, putting everything away from to-night. Wyatt asked me to come outside and wait for his dad to pick him up so we could talk some more about *it*.

"My parents say it'll be good for me. They said it's an experience, or something."

"You don't sound very excited, though."

I shrugged again. "Neither do you, and you're not the one moving."

"Hello?" Wyatt grinned, trying to lighten the mood, "you're leaving me to face all these morons *alone*", Wyatt joked, gesturing to the basement with his stick, "I won't survive without you!"

We both started laughing. I felt a little better after talking to Wyatt... it was nice knowing he'd miss me, at least.

Wyatt's dad pulled up shortly after. I waited outside until Mom was done downstairs, just thinking. My anger from earlier seemed to have calmed down a bit... maybe it was just the initial shock, or maybe I just needed someone to talk to. Mom and Dad really played this move up, like it's the best thing that will ever happen to me. And I don't doubt it'll be a good experience, but when they say things like "you can just make new friends", I always think yeah, but, it doesn't mean I won't miss my old ones. And when they say learning a new language will be cool, sure it will,

17

but it doesn't mean it won't be hard. Like, tell me it's going to be okay, but don't tell me I'm not allowed to be nervous, you know?

I kind of wish I'd said all that to Mom on the way home, but I didn't know how to bring it up. I was worried she'd think I was just being difficult again, trying to make her stay here. Truthfully, I would be quite happy if they suddenly changed their minds, but I understand that they probably won't... doesn't mean I can't hope, though.

Winter finally bloomed into spring around mid-April. Not much happened between then, save for realtor inspections and potential buyers intruding on my space almost weekly. I'd mostly managed to digest the idea that we'd be leaving in a few months, although nothing really felt quite *right* anymore. It felt like the ending credits of a good movie. It's over, technically, you're not really invested in the words on the screen. You don't take the time to read them, not that you really have time, anyway, they all scroll by so quickly. But you stick around, because maybe, just *maybe*, when the credits are over, there will be a bonus scene that gives you that closure you crave, even if you watched the movie end yourself. That's how I felt day in, day out. I lived every day just... waiting.

The house finally sold around early May. I realized then that there was nothing to hope for anymore; the deal was sealed, I only had until July. July first, to be exact, instead of celebrating our home's 146th birthday, we're moving 3'937 miles across the Atlantic Ocean to a country only known for cheese and mountains. Nice, huh?

I don't think I've ever mentioned it, but that's where Mom is from. She was born there, at least, but I'm not sure how long she actually stayed there as a kid. My grandpa was in the embassy, so they moved around a bunch. I don't really understand the specifics of how my parents met, all I know is that it was in an airport, I think Mom was visiting and then she met Dad and she just... never left. And now here we are, some fifteen years or so later, doing the opposite. It's a nice country, don't get me wrong, I've visited like, twice, I think. I might've gone when I was a baby, too, but I can't remember that. The views are pretty and it's very safe, but it always smells like manure and the people don't seem to be that friendly. Not like here, anyway. That's what worries me the most.

"Mr. Anderson", someone said.

"Oh, me too!", someone else replied.

"I got Mrs. H."

"Mrs. H? Yikes…"

Noah chuckled from behind me. "I heard Mr. Anderson lets you do whatever you want, all the time."

"Yeah, I heard you just watch movies all day", Griffin chimed in.

I totally forgot about this. Every year, when we start to close in on summer break, my school sends out a list with all the information regarding next schoolyear. That includes all the stuff about what you need to bring, room number, if anything will be different from last year and, of course, new teachers.

I never actually realized how big of a deal the switch was until I was excluded from it. In a way, I almost felt… jealous, I think, listening to my classmates rave on and on about next year. "This teacher is cool", "that teacher is cool", "this sucks", "that sucks", well to me, *everything* sucks. It sucks that I'm sitting here, in my seat, drawing spaceships in my notebook while Griffin and Noah and everyone else have something to look forward to. It sucks that I'm leaving, it sucks that I'm not as ready as I thought

I was. It sucks *so much* that it's all going by so quickly, and yet, nothing is even happening.

"...Are you okay, dude?", I suddenly heard Noah say quietly enough only I could hear. "...Did you get Mrs. H...?"

I was so lost in my own head I didn't even feel my eyes well up. Griffin shot me this sort of quizzical look, as if he didn't understand why getting Mrs. H would warrant tears but was trying to understand.

"I got her too", he said.

"Yeah, we aren't together next year", Noah said, jokingly forcing a pout, "but I'm sure she's not *that* bad."

Griffin grinned and threw his arms around Noah's shoulders, fake crying all the while laughing.

Seeing both of them joking around together like that almost stung more. I've known Noah since junior kindergarten, I don't even remember how we became friends, I swear one day we just woke up as buddies. He likes the same video game as Wyatt and I do and I'm surprised he isn't in Cubs with us, since I always thought he'd be the type of kid who'd enjoy that. Outdoorsy and all that, a bit goofy, sort of messy. He's got these big, almost buggy brown eyes and a nose that's a little too large for his snout. His hair has always been a shaggy, although thankfully in the past few years he's really grown away from the horrendous half-bowl, half-mullet cut he used to sport. All he needs to do now is learn to brush it.

Griffin is on the tall side, and by that, I mean he towers over absolutely everyone. Never in my life have I met a kid ganglier than him. Gangliness aside, all the girls in class seem to swoon a bit over him, you know, wavy hair and light green eyes. He was actually new to this school when we started back in September, but he had no issues making friends. He's a real nice kid, never gets into trouble, a bit on the quiet side but generally easy to talk to. Noah made a bromance B-line when they first met and they've been basically inseparable since.

23

I snickered a little at the sight of Griffin and Noah laugh-"sobbing" together. "I'm not in Mrs. H's class", I said with a slight smile, "thing is-"

"HA, he's with me!", Noah cut me off, swinging Griffin off his shoulders, smiling widely.

"I'm not with either of you, listen."

They straightened themselves out, looking at me with the most puzzled look.

"I'm moving."

They just stared at me, completely expressionless. They didn't say anything for about two seconds too long.

"Oh", Noah said quietly, just to say something.

Griffin mimicked quietly.

"Yeah", I said under my breath, nodding my head gently, looking away. Dang, this was a lot less awkward with

Wyatt. I can't read these two at all. Are they upset? Confused? Just trying to be polite?

"When?", Noah asked, finally.

"July first."

"Oh. That's soon."

I nodded again, swallowing the knot that was slowly forming in my throat. That *is* soon.

"Like far away, or...?" Griffin asked.

"To me it is, yeah. I'm basically moving in with my grandparents, ha-ha."

They paused again, eyed each other, and then looked back at me.

"Aren't they somewhere in Europe?" Noah said, an air of absolute bewilderment in his voice.

"Yup", I sighed.

Noah sat down on my desk silently, Griffin didn't move at all. They seemed even more shocked than Wyatt did two months ago.

"Like, forever?", Griffin's voice was abnormally timid, almost like he was worried he'd offend me.

"I mean... Probably, unless I decide to come home when I'm older? I don't really know."

"...You'll come back and visit, though?", Noah asked, inspecting the palms of his hands like he'd never seen them before.

"Of course I will, this is my home."

"Good", Noah replied. Griffin nodded in agreement, smiling slightly.

3

The weight of it all really started kicking in after that little chat with Griffin and Noah. I felt bad... first of all, the visiting thing, I mean, will they even remember me by the time I can come back? It's not like I'll settle into my new house, and then three weeks later "okay, let's go home", it doesn't work like that. It could be months, it might be years. But saying it out loud made it all feel so *real*. If I just repeat "I'm moving, I'm moving" in my head over and over again, well, it's only in my head. The things that go in my head aren't always real. But saying it out loud, *confirming* it with not one, but *two* people, technically three? That's real life. That's happening, and there is literally nothing I can do to stop it.

My parents have been becoming a little more stressed every day as they prep for the big move. I still haven't really talked to them about how I feel, every time so far I've so much as mentioned the move they start freaking out like the world is about to end. Like, okay, yeah, I'm a kid, I don't know what kind of pressure they're under... but didn't they technically sign up for this? Or is everything going wrong and they're just not saying anything about it? I'll never know, not that it matters. Not being able to talk about it is... fine, I guess. I've told Wyatt a few things and Griffin and Noah too, but I don't know if they'd really understand how I feel right now. I don't know if *I* understand how I feel right now.

It's June, already. The past three months are such a blur. So much happened, but at the same time, nothing at all. Everything had been so uncomfortably normal, save for the moments when it was so unbearably different, that I hardly even noticed the time passing and the things changing. The maple trees are thick again, casting cool shade across our driveway that radiated more heat than the surface of the sun. The park at the end of the avenue was a popular spot for mothers and daycare providers during the day, reckless teenagers at night. The city cleaned dried frogs off the bottom of the shallow concrete pool in preparation for its annual summer opening. I started to notice things I didn't notice before, and immediately regretted noticing them, worried I'll start to miss them when I leave. One more month of this, is what I keep reminding myself, until the hard part is finally over.

I expected to be more emotional come the last week of school, but I handled it surprisingly well. Between Monday and Thursday, I'll admit I barely counted as conscious, but I was definitely alive and probably somewhere between well and unwell at the very least.

Notice how I said Monday through Thursday? That's because Friday was absolute pits. It started off bad enough, I woke up on the old floor-mattress I'd called a bed for the past two weeks to find a house centipede taking a nap right beside my face. I admit, it could be worse. I could have woken up on the moon, stranded in the middle of the Sahara Desert, missing a kidney, stuff like that, but still, ew. I was fine-ish until I actually got to my bus stop and realized that this was *it*. Like, it's *over*. Bam. Just like that. This is the last time I'll see Noah. This is the last time I'll see Griffin. This is the last time I'll step foot onto the schoolyard, the last time I'll step foot *off* the school yard. All the feelings I thought I was handling well suddenly hit at once, like an asteroid of emotions crashing straight into my amygdala. The only barricade against the shockwaves was the fact that I'd see Wyatt one last time during summer, and boy was I ever glued to it.

I wrestled with myself to keep my composure during the bus ride. Thankfully I didn't have any friends on the bus, I was in one of those moods where you can save face until someone looks at your face, and I think if someone asked me if I was alright, I would've quite literally erupted into a wreck of snot and tears.

The bus pulled into the lot just as I managed to patch myself back together. By no means was I *okay*, but my emotional state was hanging on by a string instead of a thread. I decided the best course of action would be to try and make the most of my last day, spend as much time as I could with my friends and really enjoy-

"It's going to be so weird without you, dude."

Kaboom.

I didn't even manage to turn around before mucus was flowing down my face. Noah gave my back a few desperate pats and apologized profusely to try to calm me down, but the damage was done. My shoulders shook violently, people shot me side-eyes and whispered to their friends as they walked by us. This is so *embarrassing*.

"I'm– I'm fine", I just barely managed to choke between sniffs, "it's fine, everything's fine!"

"It's alright, man", Noah said, unsure of what to do, "you can cry, it's okay..."

He patted my back a few more times until I pulled myself back together. I felt like shattered porcelain held together by Elmer's glue, like the tiniest thing would set me right off again. Griffin veered around the corner as I cleared my throat, also giving my back a decided pat when he approached us.

"How are we this fine morning?", he asked us both.

Noah looked at me, then at Griffin, waiting for me to say something first. I felt my voice begin to shake before I even spoke.

"Ahem-", I cleared the tears from my throat again, "I've been better."

"I can… uh, I can see that", Griffin noted. "Is it because of the…", Griffin lowered his voice, again, almost as if he was nervous to offend me, "*the moving thing?*"

I choked on myself again, this time just barely keeping my composure, managing no more than a nod. Griffin gave me another firm, supportive pat. At least I'll have the back bruises to remember these two by.

The first bell rings at 9:00, although you aren't actually allowed inside the building yet. I never quite understood that, because then at 9:05 when the second bell rings, everyone is absolutely scrambling to get inside. It's pure chaos until you're in your classroom.

The three of us waited the line out today. We knew that one teacher would haul us over the coals for it, no idea why, she just seemed to enjoy yelling at people, but hey, this is our last day together, let's try and keep it as stress-free as possible, even if that's probably going to be impossible.

"Does talking about it make you sad?", Griffin asked as we tailed the line inside.

"Me?", I responded, having calmed down enough to speak again.

"Yeah", he looked down at his feet as we neared the stairs, "I was a little upset when I moved last year, that's why I asked."

"Yes and no? I'm not really sure what I'm feeling."

We really dragged the walk upstairs out, taking our time up each step.

"Are you excited?", Noah looked at me. For the first time since I'd known him, I think he actually might've brushed his hair this morning.

"Sure", I answered, having to think about a little bit, "I mean, yeah, I'm sad because this is my home. And you and Griffin are here, and so is everything else I know. But it's still an adventure."

Noah snickered and pursed his lips, twirling an imaginary mustache between his fingertips. "Who knows, maybe you'll replace me with a fancy European Noah."

Griffin pulled up a pair of imaginary Lederhosen, grinning from ear to ear. "You don't have to replace me, my grandma's from Germany!"

The three of us laughed as we finally approached our classroom. We kicked off our outdoor shoes and switched to our indoor sneakers before taking our seats inside. Like every morning, we start off on the carpet, where everyone sits criss-cross in a circle with our teacher in the middle.

Like every last day of school, we didn't actually do school. The morning is usually reserved for cleaning up and cleaning out, then in the afternoon we watch a movie or sing songs or something. Whatever the teacher decides is the least amount of work.

Griffin and Noah really kept me sane that morning. Once every twenty-five seconds while I was cleaning out my desk, I'd remember that this was the last time. In about half a month, I'd be 36'000 feet in the air, somewhere over the Atlantic Ocean, no turning back. Whenever one of the two noticed the glue peeling off my porcelain pieces, they'd say the stupidest thing they could think of in that moment, just to make me laugh, like asking me if I was going to learn how to yodel or take the opportunity to learn the alphorn.

I cruised through our first recess and lunch block, and scraped by our noon periods, just until I realized that the day was almost over. For the first time in my entire life, my entire school-hating… no, school-loathing life, I wasn't ready for it to be over.

4

The afternoon was such a blur of emotions. Happiness, excitement, sadness, anxiety, you name it, I felt it. Griffin and Noah talked me through all of them, although sometimes knowing that they're what I'm leaving behind made it all harder.

We hugged goodbye as the final bell rang at 3:15 in the afternoon on the concrete lot of the schoolyard, and just like that, it was over. That's why I *hate* goodbyes. All of a sudden, it's just over, and you're just supposed to be okay with that.

The last time I saw Wyatt went a lot smoother than my last day with Noah and Griffin. Maybe it's because I'd told him so long ago, I'd already managed to come to terms with it, I don't know. The last time I saw him was about a week before I left, at the last Cub meet I visited. He never mentioned the move, until the very end, when he squeezed me tight and said it wouldn't be the same without me. I wondered if he would still go to Cubs after that. He spoke to the other kids, sure, but not as often as he spoke to me. I guess it doesn't matter now, I hope he has fun at Brownsea Base. I wish we could've gone together.

The last week before leaving was the slowest waiting game of them all. Our house was packed up, as if we'd never lived there in the first place. The only remnants were my trusty floor mattress I shared with the centipedes who used to hide behind heavy furniture and the dark silhouettes of my old stuff on the faded hardwood floor.

I dragged my fingers between the cracks in the floorboards as I sat silently, listening. The moving truck had finally come to pick up the last few items we couldn't leave behind, like dad's special chair he'd sat on minimum once a day since the day I was born, shoes we wouldn't need right away, the odd trinket here and there that my parents had collected over the years, stuff like that. The sentimental things.

Dad called my name from the front door. "Cam, come out here for a minute!"

A "heatwave" can't quite describe the temperature outside. We might not have had any furniture inside, but at the very least we still had an air conditioner, and on days like today that's really the only thing you need. It was already sundown but stepping out the front door felt like walking straight into an oven regardless.

"What's up?", I asked Dad, who was looking towards the park. The pool was closed today for renovations, they actually redid the concrete just yesterday.

"What are you doing right now?", he asked me. The truck drivers closed the trailer and readied themselves to leave as we spoke.

"Nothing, I'm waiting", I answered.

"Waiting for?"

"Waiting to leave. There's nothing else to do now."

"Ah, yeah. The time will pass quickly", he assured me, "how are you feeling right now?"

"Right now? Bored."

"Bored, okay. I know this whole thing has been rough on you", Dad said, eyeing the truck drivers trying to leave the driveway that was just a tad too small for them.

"I guess it has."

The drivers finally managed to pull out, Mom sighed and quickly announced that she was going inside to cool off.

"Alright, dear", Dad waved mom off and turned to me. "Finally, everyone's gone, come with me."

Dad quite jovially made his way towards the park, a conniving grin on his face. He was up to something, but I had no clue what.

Dad stopped in front of the chain link entryway into the park, where a small patch of concrete that acted as a sort of pathway lead you straight to the pool. As much as I grew up with this park, it truly is in dire need of a makeover. Even with a "fresh" concrete landing by the entrance, it still looks equally grungy and unkept as it always has.

Dad began digging around in his pant pockets again, smiling at me wordlessly. He pulled a pocketknife from his shorts lowered himself in front of the patch, unsheathing one of the larger, more robust blades. He gently flicked his head towards the ground, signaling my queue to kneel beside him. He outstretched his left hand and grabbed my right, pulling it down towards the concrete in front of us.

My right palm made contact with the gritty paste; it was honestly one of the weirdest things I've ever felt.

Honestly, there's no every-day feeling that comes anywhere near what half-wet concrete feels like, so I'll put it like this; imagine petting a lukewarm toad with very firm back muscles, except it's been so hot the pond it lived in dried up. Put simply, gross.

Dad pushed my hand down a little deeper with the top of his left knuckles as he traced the silhouette with his pocketknife. The concrete was already semi-set, so my hand alone couldn't make any imprints worth writing home about, even if it would've been a little more charming than the blobby outline Dad was attempting to draw. Tiny rocks crunched between my splayed hand as dad dragged his knife through the grit, struggling a little bit around the tips and webs of my fingers. I lifted my hand so he could drag the final line from under my arm, connecting my thumb to my pinky, before marking the inside of the handprint with a "C".

Dad stood up, upper body bent towards the ground, and rested a hand across my shoulder blades. "There", he said, straightening himself out, "A part of you will always be here, Cameron, even if *you* aren't."

I stood up, slowly, shifting my gaze from my handprint back to the park, back to the print and back to the park again. The air smelled of pine sap and maple pollen; I guess I never really cared to notice until now, and there was a bit of a breeze. It wasn't the kind of breeze that made going out in heat like this worthwhile, but it still rustled the leaves gently as it passed through them, playing a relaxing summer melody that I always take for granted until I inevitably start to miss it, come winter. Chickadees and robins sang songs to each other from the shade of the trees; bees and other bugs buzzed around my head.

The hinges on the metal gate in front of me were all rusty; I suddenly remembered the way it would squeak whenever I opened it. The handle would jam all the time, the chain link fencing seemed to be hanging on by a thread. In the distance, the playground glowed in the sun; not because it looked good or anything, but rather because the once-yellow paint had faded to near white, reflecting the sun like a floodlight. The red accents had started to show their original iron colour underneath, funny how I never noticed sooner. From here I could already tell how the black rubber seats of the swingset would burn your butt halfway off if you sat on them. The field I used to play tag in was yellowing, like many of the lawns running the length of the avenue, struggling to keep up with the harsh summer sun.

Dad gripped my shoulder with his hand, squeezing it gently.

"Dad?", I started calmly, taking in everything around me like I'd never taken it in before.

"Yes?"

"What if I'm not happy there?"

He sighed. I worried he was about to lecture me on gratefulness and flexibility or something. "It won't be easy, son. Not in the beginning. I know it's a big change. But think of the future, the opportunities you'll have. None of your friends here will have those, that's something to be happy about."

I sighed, too, because I know Dad's right, but... he didn't really answer my question. I already know there's lots to be happy for, I keep reminding myself to be excited. But what good are future opportunities if my future isn't happy?

"And if I never start to feel at home?", I asked, hoping he'd answer this one a little better.

"Oh, Cameron. Home isn't a place. Home is wherever you make it." Dad squeezed my shoulder one last time before letting go, "come, we should go see what your mom is up to."

5

We spent the last couple of days at home seeing sights we'd already seen before. Lang Pioneer Village, the canoe museum, a walk through Jackson Park. It was a bit bittersweet, in the end. I enjoyed the daytrips for what they were but still kind of wished they weren't just to kill time until we left.

When the morning of July first finally broke, honestly, so did I. I had my moments earlier saying goodbye to my friends, but even then, I could be half-comforted by the idea that I wasn't leaving y*et*. But now, this morning? In less than twelve hours I'll already be in Toronto, probably already in the airport... maybe even in the plane. It all felt so real and not real at all at the same time.

"Good morning, Cameron!", Mom smiled at me as I zombie-walked to the kitchen. "Would you like French toast or eggs for breakfast?"

"Uh, do we still have syrup?", I asked, trying to act put-together.

"No, we just used the last of it. We have some fruit leftover, though."

"Oh, that's alright. I'll have eggs instead, please."

"Scrambled?"

"Yes, please."

Mom tipped two sunny-side-ups into dad's plate before starting mine.

"Are you ready for today, Cam?", Dad asked, peppering his eggs.

"As ready as I'll ever be", my voice was almost completely monotone, save for a slight shake.

"Come on, today will be fun. We'll go to the parade this morning, and then Debbie and her husband will pick us up and we'll all head to the airport together."

"Debbie?"

"Cameron's never met Debbie", Mom reminded Dad from the stove.

"Oh sorry, I thought you had. Well, she was a good friend back when we lived in Brampton. She offered to take us to the airport, isn't that kind of her?", he admired.

"She's coming to pick us up all the way from Toronto, just to drive back to Toronto?"

It seemed crazy to me, but hey, that's a real friend if I've ever heard of one.

Mom walked to the table and tipped some scrambled eggs into both of our plates before taking a seat on the floor next to us. Yes, we're eating on the floor. No dining table anymore. Isn't moving fun?

"Well, we haven't seen each other in a while already", she explained, "and we don't know how long it'll be until we see each other again after we've moved, so, it'll be nice to spend some time together before."

I shrugged. "Okay, yeah. That makes sense. What time is she coming?"

"She'll pick us up at around noon, we can't stay at the parade long. Hopefully we'll be in Toronto by two, our flight is at six", Dad said, shoveling half an egg into his mouth at once, "let's eat up so we can make the most of it."

Not going to lie, the parade was a bit sad. It just sucks that we missed all of the cool parts; the real fun bit doesn't happen until the afternoon, and we had to be out of there by eleven to make sure we were home for Debbie to pick us up at noon. Nevertheless, Mom tried her hardest to make the most of it and bounced around endlessly with her old mini Nikon trying to get as many pictures of me as she could, whether my ability to smile cooperated or not.

Debbie arrived perfectly on time and squeezed everyone as tight as she could, including me. She was super upbeat and bubbly, it was actually really hard to be upset when she was so giddy the whole time. Her husband didn't say too much, he just shook everyone's hand and laughed whenever Debbie did, but I liked him, too. I think two times Debbie would've been maybe a bit *too* much bubble, so he was a good counterweight to have on the two-hour drive to Toronto.

It was only about two-thirty P.M. when we arrived in Toronto, so my parents decided to grab one last meal with their friends before we parted ways. The restaurant itself was nothing special, a cute little place with a run-of-the-mill menu. We all ordered and, unsurprisingly, the conversation shifted to the move quickly. My appetite was shot, I couldn't do much but pick a little at my ravioli while my parents talked with their friends. The only thing that ran through my mind was how badly I wished I could just go *home.*

My eyes watered on and off, but I managed to choke back the tears just enough to look like I was just very drowsy. Dad kept taking sly peeks at me between popping small bites of food into his mouth and nodding along with whatever Mom was saying, as if he were waiting for the moment I suddenly collapsed into a mess of tears and emotional agony, even though I was holding myself together quite well for someone who felt like stubbing a toe would send them hurtling into a total meltdown.

By the time everyone else had finished their food, I had barely even managed a quarter of mine. I'd choked down three bites of garlic bread and a few spoonfuls of ravioli, but I felt sicker with every passing second. I dreaded what was coming next; the end-all-be-all… the final goodbye.

I attempted to stall having to say the G-word to these people by pretending I was still working through my now lukewarm ravioli, but my parents knew it was all a ruse. By the end I was practically gagging on my fork from forcing myself to keep eating, all because I wasn't sure I could handle saying goodbye to two people I don't really even know. Up until today day I hadn't had anything to do with them at all; I learned their names for the first time this morning and had exchanged maybe a sentence worth of words with them, but the idea of having to so goodbye to them felt just as bad as having to say goodbye to all my friends back home.

My parents paid the bill as a thank you to them for driving us all the way here. It was around four P.M. and high time we made our way to the airport for our flight at six. The ten-minute drive from the restaurant to Pearson was comparatively quiet to the rest of the two-hour drive from home, the atmosphere felt heavy, almost gloomy. Even Debbie's contagious happiness had dissipated into bittersweet contentedness.

My parents' friends pulled up to the waiting area to drop us off. Everyone stepped out of the car together, Debbie and her husband helped us unload our luggage from the trunk. Man, I'd been at this airport countless times before, I basically knew it inside and out like the back of my hand. It almost felt like I was going on vacation – after all, this would be a normal time of year for us to go.

"You'll keep in touch, won't you?"

"Of course we will. We'll let you two know as soon as we land."

Mom extended her arms out for a hug, gripping her friend tightly. Dad shook the husband's hand firmly and patted his left shoulder. Mom and her friend loosened their embrace, both looking over to me, before mom's friend took a few steps over and pulled me into a big bear hug.

"Stay safe", she said softly, squeezing me tightly.

My vision blurred as I shifted my gaze downwards to the concrete beneath my feet. My parents seeing me cry is one thing, but I really didn't feel like putting on a show for their friends, especially not ones I met not even half a day ago. I could feel each individual muscle in my lip quiver with what little energy my few pieces of ravioli provided, tears formed a dome over my eyes, but I was adamant not to let them fall. These people needed to hurry up and leave, pronto, before I started sniffling.

The procedure for leaving someone at the airport when you know you're probably never going to see them again was a little unclear. Eventually dad just nodded solemnly and grabbed the bigger suitcase, giving the couple one last friendly smile. I followed behind him like a little duckling, eyes very clearly drenched in tears. Mom sighed and gripped the smaller one, standing in front of her friends, just looking.

"Well... Goodbye, Deb. All the best."

"Goodbye, Manuela. Good luck."

6

The doors to the main entrance slid open, cool, dry air battling against the city's mugginess outside. I'd been to Pearson countless times before, and still, walking through those doors and into the entrance hall felt like discovering an entirely new world every single time. People from all around the globe navigated the massive interior trailing suitcases, carrying backpacks, as if it were a children's corn maze.

Still, in comparison to all the other times I'd been here, it seemed pretty empty. Maybe it had something to do with people wanting to schedule their flights for after the celebrations, maybe we just got lucky. Who knows, but it meant we were able to pretty much zip through the shorter-than-usual check-in and security lines way faster than we thought.

I was kind of just ready for this all to be over. I've waited four months for this day, constantly telling myself that when this is over, I'm home free. No more worried for the future, no more goodbyes, no more conning myself into thinking this won't actually happen and then ruining myself when it inevitably did. When I'm on that plane, everything will be okay again.

My eyes watered on and off while we waited for our flight, Dad sat next to me, tissues gripped and equipped just in case I ended up needing them. Everything, and by that, I mean me, was going relatively smoothly until the departure screen suddenly updated with a big yellow notice; our flight was delayed. Of *course* our flight was delayed. When I say we've never managed a single flight with these guys that wasn't either delayed by an absurd amount of time or cancelled entirely, I mean it, which is why it didn't come as a shock to anyone when the delay updates increased by an hour half-hourly.

I totally lost it around eleven. I was tired, uncomfortable, and genuinely just *over* this. I just wanted to go *home*. And not *get on that plane* home, I meant *go back in time home*, back in time to when I was blissfully unaware of everything that was about to unfold. I didn't care if it was March a year ago or March three minutes before that kid's dad came to pick them up; I was just sick and tired of the constant anticipation, constant anxiety, constant sadness. I was just sick and tired of *feeling*. I just wanted a break.

Dad did everything he could to calm me down, to no avail. I was truly inconsolable. Mom didn't even try, she knew there was nothing either of them could say. It was a case of letting it all out until I cried myself dry.

About an hour later I was out like a light, somehow having managed to sob myself to sleep. I wasn't really awake for the rest of the wait, or much of the flight at all. All I know

58

was that it wasn't until one A.M. that we were finally able to board the plane, *seven hours* after our scheduled departure time. My tired eyes could barely hold themselves open as we walked through the skybridge and into the plane, I remember seeing red and white lights flashing against the otherwise pitch-black tarmac outside. It would be another hour and a half sitting idly on the runway before we finally took off. At two-thirty in the morning on July second with an eight-and-a-half-hour delay, we finally left everything behind to start our new journey nearly four-thousand miles away from home.

I slept like a log for the eight hours we were in the air. I don't even think crashing in the middle of the Atlantic would have woken me up at that point, I was out like a light and not about to be switched on any time soon. It wasn't until my parents began violently shaking my as good as lifeless body and the pinging of the "fasten seat-belt" alarm started blaring in my ear did I finally come to. I felt like an old man. Every bone in my body creaked as I unglued myself from the cramped seat, I stretched my kinked neck painfully as I sat up in my seat. The air was dry, dryer than in the airport, and even colder. My ears felt blocked from the altitude but rang all the same, I straightened myself out and fastened my seatbelt. My eight-hour nap didn't help anything, if I had laid my head on any flat surface whatsoever, I would have gone right down for a second one, probably even longer than the first.

My parents occupied the isle and middle seat next to me. Mom was half-awake, I doubt dad had gotten any sleep at all over the entire flight. I looked out the porthole-shaped window at the ground below. Square fields upon square fields filled to the brim with yellow canola plants, corn stalks and some small green somethings I couldn't make out from so high up. Each plot seemed to inhabit a different slope; there was not an inch of flat land anywhere.

Hills rolled on for miles, several sprouting their own individual forests, adorned with the most adorable little farmhouses you've ever seen. The otherwise sparce decoration pulled itself tighter together as we drew nearer to the city of Zürich, although even surrounding the city itself, it seemed every square inch of land was occupied by some form of agriculture or wild forestation, like a funny little barrier meant to separate the urban from the rural. None of the plants here were dead; the sky was grey, trees a gorgeous, deep green, in the distance I could make out rain falling from the clouds above. At the very least I'd have a break from the heat.

The plane rocked back and forth with turbulence as we made our descent. The time between arriving and leaving the airport is a blur. I was so beat, I practically sleep-walked through the entire thing. All I remember from the journey is seeing my grandparents waiting for us at the airport exit, a very narrow highway, and a huge white banner pinned just under the second story window, spraypainted black with the words "*Wiuchumme Diheim*".

7

Welcome home. That's the translation. The language is a dialect of German called "Bärndütsch" that they speak in canton Bern specifically, and all 25 other cantons have their own version as well, just in case one dialect wasn't complicated enough.

I was dead-on-arrival when I walked up the wooden stairs to the second story of my grandparents' house, which was now officially our "new home". Dad followed right behind me, eyebags under his eyebags growing ever darker. We kicked off our shoes and set our suitcases in the middle of the empty hallway, silently agreeing that we'd just deal with it tomorrow.

My new bedroom was upstairs, just right of the landing, vis-à-vis the upstairs bathroom. This house is bigger than our old one, both bathrooms here are about three times the size they were back home, and even my new bedroom is bigger than my old one.

It was empty, save for an old mattress on the floor that smelled of old people, but in that moment, I couldn't have cared less and threw myself right on top of it, wrapping myself up tightly in the duvet that reeked even worse.

The next six weeks were some of the busiest in my life. Between hunting for deals on new furniture, visiting family I didn't even know I had, all the immigration stuff and getting ready to start school in a whole new country and learning a new language by scratch, I barely had any time to sit and think.

School starts in August over here, which I was a little cheesed about, knowing full well all my friends back home easily had another month of off-time. I wouldn't have minded, not really for the downtime aspect, but more because I realized I wasn't ready for school *at all*.

I'd been slowly trying to learn German with the help of a textbook meant for kids learning German as a second language, Mom and my grandma. It was an uphill battle from the get-go; there are six different ways to use the word "the" and I can't figure out any of them, not to mention how weird the sentence structure is compared to English and how stupid long and hard to pronounce all the words are. Obviously, nobody expects you to be able to learn a whole language in six weeks, but still, going to school with my A1-level German skills felt like being signed up for Tour De France after just having graduated from trike to bike.

August 12th was my first day. As far as gameplan goes, I was blank. Didn't know where anything was, who was who, didn't really understand my schedule all that well.

Mom and Dad both walked me to school on my first morning. I was so nervous I could've hurled right then and there – maybe I should've, then I could've stayed home.

They only took me up to the little pathway leading past the playground, not onto the actual schoolground itself. I could hear kids screaming and laughing, sometimes I'd catch them saying something in that funky dialect they speak here, absolutely no clue of what anything meant.

Both of my parents gave me reassuring pats before walking off the direction we came. I breathed in deeply, as deep as I could, and breathed out until I was dizzy.

I could feel eyes piercing straight through me the second I stepped on the path – I haven't even said anything yet, and I already stick out like a sore thumb, but I didn't really understand why. Am I walking weird? Are my clothes funny? Or does everyone just know each other, and can tell that I'm the new kid? I wouldn't be surprised, I mean, this school is less than a third of the size of my old one...

I lowered my head and made my way past the playground, across the tarmac and towards the main entrance.

As far as I could tell, I wasn't allowed inside yet. Nobody was lining up in front of the doors here like they did back home, but then again, it could just be too early. Just like on the playground, heads turned as I walked by; although, where on the playground the little kids were too busy having fun to care for more than a split second, the older kids over here started whispering to their buddies.

I stood by the main entrance, trying to look as normal as possible. The stares made me feel so uncomfortable, and the whispers made it that much worse. I had no clue what I was doing that was gossip-worthy, even if it *is* because I'm new, why do they care? Nobody stared and whispered when Griffin was new... plus, my parents always taught me that staring isn't polite. Is that not the norm everywhere?

I stood by the entrance, perfectly still, waiting for any sign that school would start soon. My gaze was set on the floor, hoping people would lose interest in me if I stood still, when a girl suddenly approached me.

"Kah-mé-ron?", she pointed to me.

I also pointed to me. "Cameron?"

"You are?", she asked, still pointing at me, brows furrowed. She looked to be around my age, although she was *way* shorter than anyone back home, even the girls.

"*Ja*", I said, trying to use what little German I know, "*Ich*... Um, *ich heisse*... Cameron", I struggled. My accent sounded way thicker in real-life than in any of the practice run conversations I had with Mom.

68

"Caaaaammmren?", she asked, I think trying to learn the right pronunciation. I nodded.

"I am Amélie!", she said, a grin suddenly bursting across her face. Her accent was just as thick in English as mine was in German. I smiled politely and nodded again, not knowing what else to say.

"Ähm… What class… you?", she asked, clearly struggling just as much as me.

"*Fünf*", I answered, holding up five fingers just in case, "*du?*"

"I also!", she grinned, maybe even wider than a minute earlier.

I nodded quickly and returned her smile again, before realizing that the people around us seemed to be staring and whispering even more intently than before.

Amélie suddenly gasped, as if she just found the words to say something, but the bell- er, well, it sounded more

69

like an intercom beep, but whatever it was, interrupted her. I assumed that was our queue to start lining up, so I stood back with as much discipline as I could and watched idly as everyone opened the doors and walked inside by themselves, unsupervised, in whatever order and whenever they deemed fit, looking like the world's biggest idiot.

"...You are coming?", Amélie asked, her face ripe with confusion as she held the door open for me. The few people who weren't staring before were staring now, some of them even turning their heads back with quizzical looks as they walked through the open doors.

I didn't even answer, just grunted in the affirmative and quickly shuffled inside with everyone else, cheeks hot with embarassment. We walked up to the second story and into the classroom, which was only one of two on this whole floor. Back home we had about six per floor... this school really is tiny.

Here, too, you had to switch from outdoor to indoor shoes before entering the classroom. Amélie hung up her coat on the rack while I changed shoes. She turned around and I was once again greeted by a confused face.

"Your… *Schuhe",* she explained, pointing at my shoes, "you must change."

I looked down, also confused. I did? I inspected my indoor sneakers, thinking they might have somehow gotten some dirt on them, but no, they were spotless. *"Ja… Ich habe."* I picked up my grimy outdoor sneakers to show her.

"Aha", she mumbled, replacing her sneakers with a pair of house slippers. She didn't say anything else about it, just motioned for me to follow her into the classroom.

The desks in the classroom were arranged in a U-shape with the teacher's desk in the middle by the blackboard.

I walked right past Amélie who had stopped by the teacher's desk and chose one an empty spot by the top of the U, setting my backpack down on the floor beside me.

I looked up, once again, to not a single soul's surprise, to about twenty unfamiliar faces staring at me like I'd just grown a third head, Amélie amongst them. Was it the shoes? It had to be the shoes... everyone else was wearing slippers. Like literal house slippers, some of them were even fluffy.

My teacher began walking towards me, Amélie behind her. In a panic, I prepared myself to explain the history of my indoor sneakers, and that I wasn't just a heathen who couldn't be bothered to switch shoes, but to my surprise, she was smiling.

"You must be Cameron", the teacher said, her voice soft and warm, her accent nearly nonexistent. My panic melted away instantly. She extended her right hand.

"My name is Mrs. Stadelmann, I am your teacher this year. Correct me, please, if I'm wrong: you are still learning German, yes?"

I shook her hand firmly. "I only started six weeks ago."

She nodded and smiled again before letting go of my hand and walking back to her desk at the front of the class. Her name was already written on the black board.

Amélie had already chosen a seat right next to me and was pointing at my backpack like her life depended on it. I lifted it off the floor slightly, mirroring the confused looks she'd be giving me for the past fifteen minutes. She pointed to her backpack; slung around the back of her chair, and then to my chair, which was comparatively very naked.

I looked around the classroom just to see if I understood her correctly, and what do you know, maybe floor-backpacks are a bit of faux-pas over here. Maybe

73

my classmates *weren't* staring because of my shoes...
or maybe the shoes were only half of it.

That weird intercom beep-bell sounded again, signaling
the start of the first lesson. 8:15 A.M., almost an hour
earlier than school starts back home.

8

"Nico?"

I already knew what he was going to say. He says it every time I have a presentation. Sometimes it feels like everyone magically forgets that I've only been speaking German for the past year I've been here, of course I'm still learning, and of course it's far from perfect.

"The topic you chose is pretty cool, but I couldn't understand you because of your accent. I'd try to work on that for next time."

He always says it with honey in his voice, like he's some kind of saint just trying to help me out.

My teacher, *Herr* Klausner this year, scribbled something down on his notepad before addressing Nico.

"Don't forget that Cameron has only been here for a year", he reminded Nico, "and I think you've done very well considering that, Cameron".

Nico shot me a look and turned to his friend Nevio next to him, whispering something in his ear.

This past year has been rough. Learning the ins and outs of a whole new culture has been one heck of a bumpy road, and even after all this time, I'm still not quite confident I have the hang of it. After many bouts of awkwardly walking past my teachers in the morning and getting stared at by the class, I was finally told that I'm supposed to shake their hands at the start *and* end of the day. Apparently, I'd been living the whole first week in blissful ignorance, completely disrespecting every teacher I had. I also ended up changing shoes... not for the teachers, but because I got fed-up of constantly being teased by my classmates for daring to wear sneakers instead of slippers.

"Amélie?"

"Do you still celebrate Halloween?", she asked, speaking slowly for me.

"*Ja!*", I answered. We've celebrated two Halloweens since moving here; three months after we moved was our first one, and we had the house totally decked out in all the decorations we brought from home. We ended up being the only house that decorated at all… and we only got like five or so trick-or-treaters, which kind of sucked, but oh well. I get that it isn't their culture. The second time, about four months ago, was basically the same thing, except we only got two trick-or-treaters because it was raining. "It's different here because people celebrate less. But I still enjoy it, and to me, it's still my favourite holiday."

I looked around the class for more questions, but everyone seemed to be more interested in recess.

Herr Klausner jotted something else down in his note-pad. "Okay, thank you Cameron. There's no point in starting anything else this lesson, *machemir mou Pause.*" Let's take a break.

The class slowly shuffled out of the room, Nico made it a point to gawk and whisper again. I have no clue what I did to make him dislike me, the first half year I lived here I couldn't speak to him at all, then when I slowly started to pick up the language, I only ever really talked to Amélie.

"You don't talk to Nico much, do you?", I asked Amélie once we were outside.

"Not really, no. Why?"

We walked over to the big tree by the entrance and sat down on the ring-shaped bench beneath it. It was only March, but I could already see buds on its branches. Spring comes a lot earlier here than back home.

"Eh... Nothing. *Egal.* I was just curious."

"Are you asking because of the whispering thing?"

I paused for a minute, thanking the stars that she noticed.

"I just don't get why he does it. I wouldn't say it bothers me, It's just like... *verwirrend.* Confusing. I just thought maybe you'd know if I'd done something, but I guess not. Like I said, *egal.* No big deal."

Amélie looked down to the gravel below our bench, as if there was something on her mind she didn't want to say.

"Maybe it's just... I don't know. Nevermind. Jealousy, maybe", she said, picking at her fingers.

"Jealousy? No way. What were you going to say first?", I asked. Her hesitance piqued my interest.

"Nothing. He's just a blockhead who likes to talk trash, don't worry about it."

"*Boa,* Amélie, just tell me. I won't be mad. It's not you who's being stupid."

Amélie sighed hard and rolled her eyes. "Fine. He probably thinks you're easy to make fun of. You don't fit in. And that's okay", she said, throwing her hands up in front of her defensively, "neither do I! Or I wouldn't be hanging around you."

"What?", I asked, taken aback by her answer.

"Aw, see, now you're offended. I told you it didn't matter. Forget it.", she huffed.

"No, what? What makes me an easy target? What makes me not fit in, the fact that I can't speak German?"

"Do you really need me to tell you?"

I just looked at her, my expression completely dumbfounded. Where in the world is this coming from?

"It's the fact that you're not from here."

My thoughts dried like mangoes in an oven. I misunderstood that, for sure.

"I… I am, though? I have the passport and the I.D. and everything? My mom was literally born here, she went to *Gymnasium* here, we moved here because-"

"*You* weren't born here, Cameron. You grew up half a world away. You don't make it easy for yourself either, always talking about what it's like "back home", your Halloween or whatever, the leaves, the snow, we get it. You're here now, and unless you start acting like it, you'll never fit in. You're a possum. We're martens. We just aren't the same."

81

"Oh", is all I managed to choke out in response. I didn't misunderstand.

I couldn't look her in the eyes for the rest of the day, her just sitting next to me, acting like she hadn't said anything at all, was already almost too much to handle. We've been friends for a whole year, and now, suddenly, she drops that. Did she think it was advice? Forget everything you know and love or be a target forever? How can she hear those words come out of her mouth and just be *okay* with it?

The stairs up to my house creaked as I stomped my way up and inside. Dad must've heard me elephant stepping my way home, his head was already peering out from the kitchen when I opened the front door.

"Is everything okay, son?", he asked.

"I-", my voice broke, and my knees went weak before I could even start my sentence, "I want to go home", I began sobbing.

My backpack landed with a loud thud on the floor as I ran upstairs, slamming my bedroom door behind me.

I'm a possum. I'm *just* a possum. A possum who's so pathetic he's bawling his eyes out in a bedroom he doesn't feel at home in over something someone said, something a marten certainly wouldn't do.

Dad tentatively opened my door after giving me some time to cool down, but I feigned sleep to avoid talking about it. I already knew what he was going to say. "Home is wherever you choose", "places won't make you happy", yada, yada.

I didn't go downstairs until I heard the table being set for dinner, and even then, I avoided the conversation entirely.

I struggled to sleep that night, replaying what Amélie said over and over in my head. *You're here now, start acting like it.* What exactly does "acting like it" entail? Being a butt to people because they can't speak a language like a native after only a year of learning? Or is it whispering and staring at people just because they look different, I mean, what am I, an alien? That first day they all acted like I'd just landed in my UFO and asked to be taken to their leader, when all I had was the *audacity* to walk on their pristine, previously possomless tarmac. Oh, or maybe it's expecting people to drop everything they consider important to them because it isn't a part of the marten's culture. How dare someone with a different upbringing than them step foot into their country!

I ended up thinking a lot about other interactions I'd had with people other than Amélie. They were few and far between... most people stayed out of my way entirely, especially at the beginning. I didn't speak their language, so I wasn't worth their time. The few times I tried to build bridges I got laughed at. My favourite video game? For babies. Cub scouts? Only the weird kids go scouting. Rowing? They've never been. Asking them what *they* like leads to an even deader end. They wouldn't even give me answers. Just a "you wouldn't know it, you've never heard of it, you wouldn't understand it", end of conversation.

I realized that nobody really wants to know me. Even Amélie, as much as we're friends... she doesn't like it when I talk about home. I guess it upsets her that I even refer to it as home but... sorry, I lived there for ten years. I haven't even been here two, and so far, it doesn't seem that anybody really wants me here at all.

Amélie and I only ever talk about school, and her family's farm. That's all she knows. Farming, tractors, cows, as long as it's agriculture, she knows about it. I want to talk about places I want to visit, languages I want to learn, things I want to try – but to her, she has everything she needs right here. She doesn't understand why I'd want to be anywhere else, and honestly, good for her. She knows where she belongs. But that's just... not me, and here, in this small farmer village where everyone's family trees go back five-hundred years, it almost makes me feel like a convict.

9

I shouldn't be thinking of home anymore. I'll be going into seventh grade in a few weeks, and all I can think about is home. Griffin and Noah will be switching schools, since our old elementary school only goes up to grade six. Wyatt probably started rowing with Brownsea Base, and I'm still here, alone, in my room, doodling aliens on a piece of printer paper.

I've tried to do what Amélie said and learn to "act like I live here", but if I'm being honest, I still have no clue what in the world that means. I never had to act like anything back home, I could literally just *be* and that was enough. I've been participating as much as I can in all the celebrations and traditions, I've learned about the politics and the geography and I've even joined a sports club just to try and "fit in", but it still isn't enough. It feels like everything I say is invalid unless someone who's "from here" says it too, and everything I do to fit in is trying too hard.

The sports club did help me get a bit closer to two of my classmates, Sahil and Nevio, and believe it or not, they're both friends of Nico's. I was nervous when I first noticed that they were the only two people I knew in the club, but as it turns out, we all got along just fine. Sahil and I even started walking home together afterwards.

"You know, your house is literally the coolest thing to walk past in the fall", Sahil said on one of our walks home, "Nevio and I call it the Halloween House."

We were talking about nothing in particular, just letting our thoughts run free.

"What, really? I always thought the people here didn't like it."

"Oh, they don't. But they're all sticks in the mud anyway, in fact I'm surprised Amélie is friends you."

"Ha! They really are sticks in the mud. Everything always has to be the same as it was seven-hundred years ago. I think it's silly that people like Nico don't like me just because I do things a bit differently."

"What?", Sahil asked, confusion painted all over his face.

"Nico? He's always whispering things to Nevio and making fun of my German. Amélie said it's because I'm a possum, and that makes me an easy target, or something."

Sahil groaned, rolling his eyes. "Amélie *would* say that."

"…Is that not what's going on?"

"Cam... I'm a mouse. Nevio is a porcupine. Why would Nico go after you for being a possum but not us?", he asked. It was clear he wasn't angry at me, but at what Amélie said.

I felt so dumb in that moment. Somehow in my desperate search for a reason, I completely blazed over the fact that both Sahil and Nevio stick out like sore thumbs. Sahil's short and bony, all of his clothes hang off of him like bedsheets because he can't find anything small enough. His ears are almost too big for his head, and his spattered with caramel-coloured freckles that really pop against his dark brown fur.

Nevio is the exact opposite; he's huge. He's the tallest in the class, has golden-tipped quills running down the length of his broad back and has claws so long his fingers look like swords, but his gentle face doesn't seem to match his otherwise intimidating image at all.

"Then what are all those stupid comments about my German about? And all the whispering whenever I say something?"

"Look, Nico is… a bit… insecure. To him, not speaking German perfectly is a lip he can dig his claws under. It makes him feel big. But I think dumping on you because you're a possum is a step too far, even for him."

"Oh."

I almost didn't want to ask about Amélie, but I knew the question would eat me up inside forever if I didn't.

"What's the deal with Amélie?", I asked, hesitantly.

"I'm surprised you never noticed anything", he said, smiling nervously, "don't take this the wrong way, 'cause I know you're friends and I'm sure she's real nice to you, but Amélie just has a few… special ideas."

"Special ideas?"

"About people like us."

"Like you and me?"

"Maybe just Nevio and I, if she's friends with you."

It took me a while to get what Sahil meant, he was being a bit cryptic, like he didn't want to badmouth Amélie in front of me. Then I remembered what she said, about being an easy target, just because I'm not from here. My passport not being worth the same because I wasn't born here. *My* Halloween. *My* leaves. *My* snow.

The idea that I had been friends with her for so long without even thinking twice about it made me shiver. It's not even that Amélie says things like that out of insecurity like Nico, because at least that I could pity; no, she says that because she *thinks* that. How can you think something like that?

I spent the rest of my summer break thinking, rethinking, and overthinking everything. Sahil and Nevio were both born here, Nevio even has a passport, and his first language is German. Sahil doesn't have a passport, but you wouldn't know his first language isn't German unless he told you. If you think about it like that then I'm the most alien of all of us and yet, I'm the one that Amélie is okay with. I just don't get it.

My first day of seventh grade was so nervewracking. Over here, the classes in seventh grade get mixed into three groups of three grades, so three different homerooms made of seventh through ninth graders. I don't know why it's done like that, and I don't know if it's the same everywhere or just at my school, but it basically means that instead of having one little class that you know and spend all your time with, you end up spending a little bit of time with basically everyone in the entire seventh through ninth cycle.

I ended up being sorted into homeroom three with Nico, Nevio, and thankfully, Sahil. Amélie was in homeroom one, not that it mattered. We'd still have all our core subjects together and a few others.

By day one, things were already going south. We had two teachers, one of which nobody knew yet. She was new and obviously excited to start teaching, Frau Gersbach. The other one had a bit of a reputation for being… unpleasant, and man, did she ever look like it. Her name was Frau Tarkovskya, although as far as anyone could tell, she wasn't Russian. The two looked like polar opposites of each other. Frau Gersbach was always dressed in bright colours, sporting the biggest smile she could, and seemed genuinely interested in all of us. I think Frau Tarkovskya regretted every life choice that led to her being a teacher.

On the first day, we were mixed into learning groups that were supposed to help us get to know each other a bit, so none of us seventh graders were in the same one.

I was with two ninth graders and an eighth grader, none of whom I'd ever met before.

"What exactly are we supposed to be doing? I wasn't listening", one of the ninth graders said.

"Read the paper, nitwit", the eighth grader replied, shoving a paper in his direction. We were sat facing each other around a square table, a side for each of us.

The other ninth grader grabbed a pencil from her case and began writing everyone's names on an empty sheet of graph paper, stopping before mine.

"I'm sorry, uh, I don't know your name", she said.

"Cameron."

She looked at me with wide eyes, deciding to write a "C" on the paper instead.

"What is that, like, American or something?", the eighth grader asked, his left arm slung over the back of his chair.

"I think it's technically scottish, but yeah it's pretty popular all around North America."

He nodded before hunching over the paper, losing interest in me completely. "All right... First question. How big is the country's area in square kilometers?"

"Pffffshh, small. Like thirty thousand", one of the ninth graders said.

"No, it's a little bigger. Write fourty-nine thousand", the other one corrected.

"It's roughly fourty-one thousand", I said. It was written in the German book I used to learn with, so I was confident I was right.

My groupmates all looked up at me but didn't say anything. The eight-grade and ninth-grade boys looked to each other wordlessly, before scribbling down the answer fourty-nine thousand.

"Okay, next question", the other ninth grader said, moving on, "what is the capital of Ticino?"

"Lugano", both boys said simultanously.

"Bellinzona", I answered.

"Lugano is bigger than Bellinzona", the eighth grader argued.

I shrugged. "Zürich is bigger than Bern but Bern's still the capital of the country."

"How would you even know that?", the ninth-grade boy suddenly prodded.

"What?"

"Stuff about capitals. Haven't you only been here for like, a year?", he asked.

"Two", I answered, trying to keep my voice still.

The eighth grader started laughing. "Kid's been here for three days and thinks he knows things", he taunted.

"Man, leave him be, he's not hurting you", the ninth-grade girl suddenly stopped them both, "who knows, maybe Stars n' Stripes is actually right."

I slumped down into my seat, completely humiliated. The other groups seemed to be doing just fine, especially Nico's. They were all laughing and smiling, and here I wished I could just disappear. I mean, Stars n' Stripes? Really? I'm not even American. If I had told them where I'm from, it would've been another case of me "not acting" like I'm from here, I'm sure.

"Alright, is everyone through with the questions?", Frau Tarkovskya asked the class in her usual bleak tone.

My groupmates had just finished scribbling down another answer, I don't know to which question, I don't care. Whatever I said wouldn't be right, anyway.

"All done", our eighth grader said, all the other groups following suit.

"Alright, question one, area in kilometers. Can someone answer?"

None of my groupmates raised their hands, I didn't have the guts to, either. If I was wrong, I'd never hear the end of it.

Frau Tarkovskya pointed to one of our groups and nodded halfheartedly, like she didn't really care.

"Fourty-one thousand kilometers?"

"Good", she answered, "next one: capital of Ticino."

Our eighth grader raised his hand. "Lugano?"

"No, any other ideas?"

He hesitated for a second. "…Bellinzona?"

"Yes, exactly."

All my groupmates were suddenly quiet, fiddling with their hands or pencils or whatever was near them.

The third question was national history, when was the country founded. August 1, 1291. I know that, too, and once again the answer they had written down on their paper was wrong.

I was livid for the rest of the day. Sahil commiserated with me on the way home, it felt nice to have someone who understood. Amélie had tried to sweep it under the rug a bit, claiming they must've just been trying to "keep an image". Some image they kept.

I dinosaur trotted upstairs, grumpy as ever. Mom and dad were both home already, chit-chatting in the living room.

"Hello?", Dad called from the living room as I opened the front door.

"It's me", I grumbled.

"Uh-oh. What's wrong, Cam?"

I swallowed the urge to whine about wanting to go home and tried to stay calm while explaining what happened.

"My new classmates are just stupid."

"Why are they stupid, Cam?", Mom asked, putting her phone on the coffee table.

I fell onto the couch, stiff as a board, arms crossed.

"They just are. We had to answer questions in groups, and they didn't listen to me at all. They said I don't know anything because I haven't been here long enough. All my answers were right! Theirs were all wrong!"

"What?", Dad was bent forward in his chair, looking angrier than I'd seen him in a while, "No, that's unacceptable. They ostracized you for something silly like that?"

I nodded, not knowing what else to say. It sounded a lot worse when Dad used the word ostracize.

"That's unbelievable. I'm going to write a letter to your teacher."

"What? No, no, it's fine, it's not that bad", I freaked out. It was just one bad day out of a whole year, writing to my teachers would make me look like a baby, and what if it got out to my classmates? I'd be done for.

"Sorry Cam, but I can't let that slide. Behaviour like that is simply unacceptable. I'll write her a letter tonight."

"Good. What brats are they. I can't believe that, not one bit", Dad said.

Shoot. I shouldn't have opened my mouth. I should've just let it go. My life is over.

10

"These learning groups just aren't working, we have to change them", Frau Tarkovskya said in her usual dull, done-with-life tone.

Mom sent an e-mail last night. I have no idea what was in it, all she would say was that I didn't need to worry about it and "she'd sort it out". Well now I'm sitting at the back of the class, right in the middle of everyone, sweating buckets.

"Why?", someone shouted.

"They're just not working", Frau Tarkovskya repeated. looking right at me. Don't you say it, don't you dare say it.

"There's got to be a better reason than that", someone else said.

There isn't a better reason, don't say it, don't say-

"Cameron feels left out."

I felt everyone's gaze shift onto me at once, my heart pounding straight out of my chest, sheer embarassment and humiliation washing over me like a tsunami. Is that kind of stuff not confidential? Is she allowed to say that?

I wanted to disappear, to disintegrate into a million tiny pieces. This isn't real. There is no way this is happening. I didn't have the guts to look up from my lap, I stayed still like a guilty puppy, hoping I'd suddenly wake up to realize it was all some horrible nightmare. They were already whispering, I didn't know who, it didn't matter. Everyone will know by tomorrow anyway.

"So, uhh… Yeah. Let's switch these groups up, shall we?", Frau Tarkovskya said, attempting and failing to diffuse the tension. This woman is so awkward, honestly, she pulls something like that and then just moves on? "Oopsie, I ruined your life. Welp! Anyway", like, what?

My new group consisted of another two people I didn't know, and just in case I hadn't been given enough cosmic punishment: Nico, wearing a super-sized fish-eating grin on his face. This must be the best day of his sorry little life. I bet he feels *huge*.

I couldn't look at anyone for the rest of the lesson, let alone speak. Stares burned right through my mind, whispers sounded like shrieks, the only thought that managed to run through my mind was a helpless plea from a boy who wishes he had never come here in the first place. I want to go home, let me go home, I *need* to go home.

I was the last person to leave the classroom in an attempt to preserve what little dignity I had left. Next is English, that's fine, I'm good at English. I'm the best at English. Everything is okay.

"You look a little flustered, Clammy." Nico's grin was easily a foot wider than it was before. Sahil and Nevio were by his side, both wearing the most pitiful expressions they owned.

"That whole thing was an accident, I swear. That teacher is such a-"

"You're so embarassing, Cameron. You'll never come back from this, you know that?"

"What the heck, man, this literally isn't my fault, I-"

"Everyone's going to find out about this. You'll be the talk of the town! That's what you want, isn't it?"

"Would you shut up?"

"*Ih bi froh bini nid di.*" I'm glad I'm not you.

Nico turned around before I could say anything else, Nevio following close behind.

"Do you wanna go to the bathroom for a minute?", Sahil suggested once Nico was out of earshot.

I nodded, feeling a lump form in my throat.

Sahil ran one of the taps as soon as we entered the bathroom.

"Rub your face down, it might make you feel a bit better", he said, "Nico's just blowing this all out of proportion. In three days, nobody will care."

I closed the tap, resting my cold hands over my eyes.

"And if they do?", I asked, trying to keep myself together.

"I won't care."

"You'll chew your reputation to bits, hanging out with a quack like me."

Sahil laughed quietly, calmly, like he knew everything would be fine.

"I'm a mouse, Cam, in a country full of martens. I've always been at the bottom of the food chain."

I was right. Everyone knew about what happened by the following day; and the day after that, there were already nine different variations of the same story.

There's no use trying to salvage anything, not that there's anything left to salvage. Nico's got what he always wanted; to feel big. He's the biggest kid in school right now, he controls the news. The rumours. His claws are sunk deep into me, and I have no idea how to get them out.

It was fine when it was just him, it's not just him anymore now, though, it's all these people who don't even know me. Who don't *want* to know me because it's fun to have someone to kick.

The things they say have gotten meaner, too. It isn't just about my German anymore. It's the way I look, the way my voice sounds, the way I walk. They get their hands on everything they know is dear to me and rip to shreds, just for fun. Old topics even I had forgotten about are suddenly brought up again, just because they can, just so they can hurt me.

"It's just weird to me, that's why I don't really understand it", Amélie said. The leaves were slowly starting to brown and fall, it didn't look quite as pretty as it does back home, but fall is still my favourite season, even here.

Amélie was sitting on the swing, slowly rocking herself back and forth. I was in the tire swing next to her, my butt halfway touching the floor.

"I don't get what part you don't get!", I said, exasperated. I've been trying to explain what started this whole thing all day, but Amélie just won't grasp it.

"I don't get why they'd just start ganging up on you about not knowing stuff. That doesn't make sense to me."

"What, and you think it makes sense to *me*? I was the punching bag, not the boxer."

"Don't you think you might have just… overreacted a bit?"

"What?"

"I don't know, I'm trying to make sense of it all. Maybe they were just joking?"

"…Joking?"

"Yeah. And it just didn't land, I mean, your German isn't perfect, and…"

"And that means absolutely all of the revolting things they've said to me are entirely justified?"

"Oh my gosh, Cameron, calm down. You *want* to be angry. You know not everyone in this country is a monster trying to tear you down? We don't all root for your failure, you know", Amélie said, then mumbled something under her breath.

"What was that?"

"Nothing."

"Say it."

"No, because then I'll be the evil marten who hates you because you're a possum again."

"Well, when you say it like that-"

"You've been hanging around Sahil too much."

"What does Sahil have to do with anything?"

"Jeez, Cameron, if you wanted me to paint a freaking picture you should've brought an easel. He's brainwashed you into thinking we're all awful and want the worst for people like you."

"People like me? What's the difference between people like me, and people like you?"

"Cameron, stop."

"What's the difference?"

"Enough, stop, this is stupid. You're right, your classmates acted dumb. Happy now?"

My fists were wrapped around the ropes of the tire swing so hard they burned. Who does this girl think she is?

"No, tell me the freaking difference", I seethed through gritted teeth.

Amélie sighed, loosening her tense shoulders for just a second, her upper body turned away from me. She shook her head before finally looking in my direction, but not at me.

"People like *me* belong here, Cameron. If you *foreigners* hate it here so much, why don't you do *everyone* a favour and go back to wherever it is you came from?"

I pulled myself out of the tire before Amélie had even finished her sentence.

"If I could, I would."

11

"Namaste, Sahil", one of our classmates mocked, bowing down as he walked by Sahil's seat.

"Nama-stay away from me", Sahil mumbled.

"Don't even bother, dude, these jerks get a kick out of your reaction", I said to him.

"They're not even doing it right!"

"Do you really think they care?"

Sahil sighed, resting his chin on his desk.

We haven't been able to catch a break since this all started, and it's always the same stupid jokes they make over, and over, and over again. It's not even just limited to us, anymore. Nevio's been put through the wringer more times than I count, but he just lets everyone do it. They'll tear him down for the way he looks, things that he has absolutely no control over. I've watched people literally move away when he sits down next to them and start loudly mocking him for his size, his quills, his claws, and he just sits there and takes it with a smile. Even Nico, his "best friend", has started saying things Sahil was certain he never would, awful things, things I know hurt like knives in Nevio's back.

You'd think that since he knows how it feels, he wouldn't put us through the same thing. I could see the devastation on Sahil's face the first time Nevio loudly excalimed that he reeked of curry when he walked into class after lunch. It's embarassing, almost, because inevitably those nitwits will just turn it back around on Nevio right after, but I get it. When you feel as small as the three of us do, you'd do anything to feel big, even if it's only for a moment.

I crossed my arms over my desk next to Sahil and burried my face. Everything has been so, so hard since we came here. Mom and Dad promised me opportunities, and benefits, and friends before we came here, well look where I am now. Exhausted and ready to give up, missing people who probably forgot they even knew me once, yearning for a feeling I haven't felt since we left the avenue.

I don't belong here. I'll never belong here, not for as long as everyone who does keeps hammering it into my mind.

"What's the deal between you and Amélie?", Sahil asked out of the blue.

"Um, nothing. We had a bit of an argument", I answered.

"Just an argument? Really?", he sounded surprised.

"Yup, really. That's all."

"Must've been a little than a bit of an argument… Look at the way she's looking at us", he said quietly, fixing his posture, "that girl has purgatory in her eyes."

I chuckled at his description, it was spot on. Amélie had texted me a few times after the fact, but I never replied. There is no coming back from what she said, not just to me, but about all of us. Us "foreigners".

So far, the only good part about having moved here is the fact that I have Wednesday afternoon off. Sure, Wyatt, Griffin, Noah, and everyone else must be having a blast back home, making friends, trying new things, not having to fight tooth and nail for the right to be seen as more than just a foreigner, but do they have Wednesday afternoons off? Doubt it.

"I'm home", I said, walking through the front door on a crisp November afternoon. It's probably already snowing back home, but here, it's still warm enough to walk around in just a sweater.

"Hi, son", dad answered from the living room, "how was your day?"

I threw myself down into the couch, letting the seats swallow me whole. "Fine."

"Just fine?", Dad asked.

"Yeah."

"Nothing new and different?"

"No."

"Fine", Dad huffed.

"So, Cameron, have you thought about what you want to do after school?", Mom asked, peeling herself away from her magazine.

The familiar urge to say "go home" ran through my body like an electric current, but once again, I pushed it down.

"I was thinking maybe Gymnasium", I said instead. That wasn't true, though, I hadn't been thinking about it at all. I was just tired of not having a good answer when people asked.

"Gymnasium?", Mom's said, shocked, "do you have any idea how hard that'll be?"

"Pretty hard, probably."

"*Very* hard, Cameron. Why don't you do an apprentice-ship instead?", she suggested.

"As what?"

"Well, what interests you?"

I thought about it for a second, before concluding that nothing brings me joy anymore.

"I don't know. That's why I said Gymnasium, so I'll have four more years to figure it out."

"But son, if you did an apprenticeship, you'd have a profession as soon as you're done. You'll be wanted across the whole country, and then if you want to change career paths afterwards, you still can", Dad said.

"But I wouldn't have a diploma."

"What do you need a diploma for? Nobody will care about that here."

"And if I don't want to stay here?", I said, looking at him dead in the eyes. I hate discussions about the future, they always end the same. My parents just assume I'll stay in this miserable little pigpen of a village in the buttcrack of nowhere until I'm old and grey, granted the farmers don't exile me first.

"Where else would you want to be? You have so many opportunities here, with you speaking French, English *and* German, people will be picking you up left and right."

"Home?", I snapped, "literally everyone speaks those languages over here, they'll replace me with some moron named Ruedi the second they get the chance."

"What in the world are you talking about?", Mom asked, her tone an uncomfortable mix of offended and angry.

"The grass is always greener, Cameron, if you're miserable here, you'll be even more miserable there, but hey, it's not my life", Dad said, looking down at his tablet.

An answer like that usually meant he'd checked out of the discussion. I dropped the whole thing and went up to my room instead.

I texted Sahil, asking him to come outside with me for a bit. There was nothing specific I wanted to talk about, I just didn't want to be in my house.

"Everything okay?", he asked as I greeted him from my driveway.

We started walking. There's nowhere to go in this village but straight, so that's where we went.

"Ahh, yeah, probably. I got into another argument with my parents, I just wanted to get out of the house for a bit."

"Aw, I'm sorry, Cam. What about?"

"Real stupid stuff. My future and staying here."

"That doesn't sound stupid to me. Your parents want you to stay here or what?"

"I dunno. They just think it's better for me here. They say it like it's a suggestion, but the kind of suggestion I don't have a choice in following through with."

"…Do they know about everything that's going on at school?", Sahil asked, tentatively, as if he was worried he'd offend me. It reminded me of Griffin, a little.

"Phew… I mean, they know a little bit. I tried to explain it to them at the beginning, but I don't think it really clicked why I was so upset. They think I'm making it out to be worse than it is."

"What? Why?"

"Attention."

"Attention? The whole problem is that we get too much of it."

I like the way Sahil grumbles with me. I've never needed to explain anything to him, I can just say words and he'll put them together in the right order. He just… gets it. He gets me. As much as literally everything is the pits right now, knowing that there's at least one person by my side who gets it effortlessly, makes everything just a tiny bit better.

We walked up one of the hills overlooking the valley. There's a maple tree up top; one of the only ones in the whole valley, tucked away neatly in between two fields. You can see the whole village from up here, the sun sets on the opposite side of the valley, and on sunny fall evenings like today, there aren't many spots that come close to this one.

I threw my jacket on the grass beneath the maple tree and collapsed on top of it, enjoying the silence. Sahil laid his jacket on the grass next to mine and sprawled out beside me.

"Back home this tree would already be naked", I said, looking up at the maple above us. It was about half as thick as it was when I last visited during the summer, but still wore plenty of gorgeous orange leaves on its crown.

125

"Can I ask you something?", Sahil said, eyes closed. He looked relaxed like an old man taking a nap.

"Go ahead", I answered.

"When you're home… like, in your house home, in your bed, or whatever your favourite spot is… do you feel like you're home?"

"…No."

"Huh."

Sahil paused.

"Me neither", he said quietly. "Cam?"

"Yeah?"

"What does it feel like to belong somewhere?"

"It feels… easy. Like no matter what you say, your people will be all ears. They'll do their best to understand you, if they don't already, and when you have disagreements, you set your differences aside and work through them together. You don't feel judged, you don't feel the need to impress anyone, you can just be… you, at your worst, at your best, however you are, and know someone will always have your back."

"Oh", he paused again, "can I say something mushy?"

"Sure."

"That sounds like you."

12

"I still can't believe we did it", I said to Sahil, sitting across from me in the bus.

"It hasn't hit me yet, either", he said, smiling wider than I'd ever seen him smile before.

We did it. Nobody thought we would, but hey, hard work pays off, and now today's our first day at Gymnasium, the most academically challenging institute in the country pre-University. When we graduate from here, we'll be allowed to enroll in almost any university Europe-wide, and depending on the country, outside of Europe too.

I wish I could say the end of grade school went out with some big bang, and everyone realized that what they were doing was wrong; but in the end, they just lost interest when they realized that Sahil and I weren't letting it bother us anymore. Every now and again they'd still grapple at the mistakes I made in German or say something stupid about things Sahil and I celebrate or even something stupid about us as people, but it wasn't a constant, soul-sucking barrage of ignorant comments about where we came from or what our places here are.

The one thing we weren't expecting was for Nevio to want to go to Gymnasium, too. It was odd, seeing him there next to us when the teacher told us all we'd made it, but hey, good for him. By some miracle Sahil and I are still together in the same class, but Nevio isn't.

"Things will be different this time, I'm sure of it", I said, hoping my optimism would be enough to make my wish come true.

"They will. This time, nothing can hurt us. It's a fresh start."

The bus pulled into the train station the of town next door, about a fifteen-minute ride from our village. It acts as the main hub for the whole region, and even with only roughly fifteen-thousand inhabitants, it's the biggest town in the area.

"Um... how exactly do we get to school from here?", I asked, realizing I had forgotten to check beforehand.

"I think... I think it's just straight ahead. Let's go straight and hope for the best."

"Sahil, Cameron", a deep voice suddenly sounded from behind us, "could I walk with you two?"

Sahil and I looked over our shoulders, to each other, and then over our shoulders again.

"I... guess?", Sahil answered, looking at me for moral support.

"Thank you", Nevio smiled.

We walked through the underpass of the station in awkward silence, Sahil and I at a total loss for words. We communicated silently through looks, both asking the same question: *what?*

"So… uhh… you nervous?", I awkwardly asked Nevio, who was still walking a few steps behind us.

"A little, sure. New school", he answered coolly.

"Yeah, I get that", I said, looking at the ground.

Awkward silence.

"What *Schwerpunktfach* did you choose?", I asked.

"My focal subject is law and business."

"Cool, cool. Ours is biochemistry."

"Nice."

Awkward silence.

"…How's Nico?", I asked, grasping at straws.

Nevio sighed from what I assume must've been the deepest part of his lungs. "We... don't talk anymore. Fresh start, like Sahil said in the bus."

"Oh, wow. I'm sorry to hear that."

I looked over to Sahil, who silently returned my surprised expression.

"That's actually kind of why I asked to walk with you two, um... I'm sorry."

"Oh", Sahil and I said in unison.

"For everything, really, I am. I know it isn't an excuse but it's just... for as long as I can remember, it was always me who was the butt of all their jokes. I saw a chance to finally be on their level and I took it without even thinking. We were really awful to you both."
"Yeah, kinda", I answered.

Sahil rolled his eyes at me. "You did realize that it didn't make you any bigger though, right? They didn't see you any differently, Nevio, they just had more tar-gets."

"I know, I know, I'm sorry. I just didn't want to start this year without saying something first. I want to do better."

Sahil and I looked at each other again, I shrugged.

"Like I said in the bus… it's a fresh start. For all of us", Sahil said.

"No hard feelings, Nevio", I agreed.

"Thank you, both of you."

"It doesn't have to make us friends", I said as Sahil and I walked into our new classroom.

"No, I know, but still. It was just odd, is all, after all this time."

"I agree, but hey, he apologized. That's what matters."

Sahil looked around the empty room, deciding to sit in the same spot we sat in at our old school, the back right corner of the U.

We watched people slowly start to fill up the room, nod-smiling at all the people who looked at us. I could already tell things would be different this year – these kids look *fancy*. Like, polo shirts and expensive jeans fancy, not farmer chic.

That, and the fact that the number of not-martens was almost the same as martens. These kids come from all over the place, and I think quite a few of them already know each other.

We were sceptical at first, but these people really are *completely* different than our old schoolmates. Everyone was very reserved at first, keeping to the cliques they already knew – but as soon as our teachers started mixing us into groups with people we'd never spoken to before, it's almost as if we'd all gone to school together since we were kindergarteners.

"So, you all moved here, then?", I asked our new group over lunch.

"I was four, yup!", one of the girls, Amisa, answered. She was one of the shyer few at the beginning, but once you get to know her, she's a total chatterbox. She's always laughing at something, usually herself, and so keen to learn about… well, everything.

"I was born here, actually", Shahid replied. He's a friend of Amisa's, and very quiet, but he's one of those people that never speaks, and when they do, you're completely bewildered by how knowledgeable they are.

"I was too", Sahil smiled at Shahid.

"My family's literally never moved from here so I obviously was too", Mara answered. Also a friend of

Amisa's, as far as I know they used to be in the same class at their old school. Mara is also a little on the quieter side, less so than Shahid, moreso than Amisa. She's very sweet and is the type of person to want to hear all sides of a story before deciding what's right.

"Yup, same." Florian's the only one who was chatty from the get-go. He's definitely more... uh, posh, than any of the other kids I've met from this country. He only drinks sparkling water and doesn't like chocolate, can read a 600-pager in a day and is always up to date with whatever is trending. He's the world's biggest mythology buff and could rave on and on about the ancient Greek for hours.

"I was fourteen", Melina answered.

"Fourteen? Holy smokes", I said, taken aback, "I struggled with being ten... how in the world did you manage that?"

Melina is the quietest out all our new friends. She only speaks when spoken to, gets nervous looking people in their eyes and talks in a pseudo-whisper.

"All it is, is hard work", she explained, "everyone said I would never make it."

"Oh yeah, we've been there", I said, smiling.

"YES, same, and like, I was four when I moved here. That's a normal age to start school, like… why would I be struggling? I was a little kid, I learned German in a year or something", Amisa mentioned.
"Me too! And I didn't even move here, I just don't speak German at home", Sahil agreed.

"I never understood people like that", Florian said, "I'm an *Eidgenoss* through and through. I don't have a drop of any other blood in me, and to be honest, I don't think my German grammar improved past second grade, but nobody ever said anything like that to me."

Amisa could barely contain her laughter at Florian's comment. "That's just the way things are, and it sucks to hear it, especially as a little kid. The people who say it are usually the people who are supposed to motivate us to do better."

"But it makes all of our successes feel so much sweeter", Shahid said.

I looked at Sahil beside me. He was smiling from ear to ear, his braces gleaming with all the sunlight they were getting. I couldn't help but  smile too, seeing him beam like this, for the first time since I'd met him. *This* is what it feels like to belong. No judgement, no one-upping each other's stories or trying to be the best. Just people who get each other; and the few who don't try their best to understand anyway.

13

Everyone told me this whole Gymnasium thing would be hard, but to be honest, life has never been this easy. I got used to it always being Sahil and I against the world, and now all of a sudden, out of nowhere, we've found a whole group of people who understand everything we've been through perfectly.

We all come from wildly different walks of life, some of us fled our homes for safety, some in search of a better life, some have always been here, and some are here just because. Despite those differences, we can all relate to each other in some way or the other. It's a feeling I really hope everyone gets to experience at some point in their lives.

There is one thing that makes me a bit jealous, though. Except for Melina, and obviously me, everyone else still goes home. Sahil goes to see his family ever few summers, Amisa goes almost every time we have a break from school, and Shahid goes every now and again, too. They always come back and have the coolest stories to tell, memories they want to share with everyone, news about what's changed since last time, and every time, Melina and I are just kind of... there. We'll listen happily, of course, but I can see it on her face, too; it stings a little bit.

I haven't stopped thinking about all my friends back him since I left. By now it's been seven years, I *know* I should have forgotten about them, probably a long time ago. The odds of them remembering about me are as good as null; or at least, that's what I thought.

I remember the date, even. October nineteenth. Notice how all the good things in my life always seem to happen in the fall? There's a reason I like it so much.

Everything started off normally that day. I walked into chemistry half-alive at 7:30 A.M., sat myself down next to Sahil and nearly fell back to sleep the second my butt made contact with the chair. The leaves under the shelter above the walkways between buildings started shifting from their deep summer green to a mix to a pretty, reddish-rusty brown. Chemistry dragged on the same way it always does, I regret chosing biochemistry as my focal subject, but oh well, everyone makes mistakes.

The bell ringing after what feels like a full day always sounds just like an angel singing from the heavens, announcing the end of our chemistry period. I packed my things and took a quick peek at my phone. A notification from one of my social media accounts caught my eye, but in the haste of switching classrooms, I decided to leave it for later. I put my phone back in my pocket and made my way down to the test hall for English.

An English test basically means a free period for me. We have forty-five minutes to an hour to finish them depending on how hard they are, but I'm usually out of the room fifteen or so minutes early and use the rest of the time to do some last-minute homework or whatever there is to do.

Like usual, I handed in my test with about fifteen minutes to spare and left to go wait in our regular English room, pulling out my earbuds and phone on the way out. I exited the test hall and made my way down the walkway, admiring the leaves overhead. I turned my phone on and remembered that notification from earlier, deciding I wasn't doing anything worth leaving whoever it was on delivered for. I slid up on the notification and instantly felt a shockwave of surprise pulse through my stomach, stopping me dead in my tracks. It

143

wasn't a message – it was a friend request. From *Noah.* *The* Noah? From all those years ago? I couldn't believe my eyes; did I really read that right? *Noah?* Maybe it was just some guy with the same first name, it's not like that's an uncommon occurrence. I know at least four different Noas – albeit spelled without an H, and he had the right last name. The second I saw one of his pictures, though, there was nobody else it could be. He had the same messy, long hair, square jaw, big brown eyes. He even dressed the same, funny enough. It really was him. *The* Noah.

I accepted his request and sent him one back, trying not to get too excited. There's got to be a reasonable, logical explanation for this, like some crazy coincidence or maybe he's a secret Doppelgänger and I'm psyching myself out over nothing.

"What's up with you?", Sahil asked, walking into the English room, "you're all smiley."

"I got a friend request", I answered.

"That's a lonely man answer", Sahil joked, jumping over the desk in front of him, "who from?"

"Noah."

"Wow! I don't know who that is."

"An old friend of mine, from back home. We haven't spoken since I left… and now all of a sudden, he's sent me a friend request."

"That's super weird, but also super cool. Maybe he just remembered your name, or something, and thought he'd reach out? You should text him."

Our other classmates slowly began filing into the English room.

"I don't know, I don't know what I'd say. I'll give it a think", I decided.

"Sure, man, do whatever you want. But I can't imagine anyone would reach out after seven years just because why not. Your buddy probably doesn't know what to say, either."

I spent the rest of the day thinking of things to say. Everything that came to mind felt so awkward, so forced, and I worried that if I dared send any of my provisional texts, I'd scare Noah away before we even had a chance to reconnect.

My lucky break came in the evening when I opened that same app to see that Noah had posted something – a video of Noah playing around on a slackline in front of a beautiful backdrop of browning trees, fallen leaves, the alps, and- wait a minute, *the alps*?

My brain short circuited for a moment. I replayed the video and noticed the location tag – *Interlaken.* A city not even two hours from where I live.

The gears in my brain were spinning at the speed of light, everything that popped into my mind stuck for only a second before being replaced by something else. My brain simply couldn't compute. Is this real life? Did I read the tag wrong? Is this guy actually a Doppelgänger who happens to live in Interlaken or is October officially my lucky month?

I decided it was now or never. I clicked the button to send him a message and wrote the simplest, world's most boring, but safest message I could think of.

> Hey, is there any chance we used to go to school together?

> Hey, yeah, we did! I remembered you moved here, just thought I'd see if you still remembered me :)

Surreality just became reality. After spending seven years convincing myself he had long forgotten, here he is, practically on my freaking doorstep. And even if he's here by coincidence... he still remembered. He still remember*s*.

We made a bit of smalltalk, I found out Noah had graduated a few months ago and was on a backpacking trip through Europe, he decided to stop by on a whim. He was only going to be here for another two days, meaning I really had to wrap this whole meeting up thing up.

Hey, they say you miss one hundred percent of the shots you don't take. Even a shot in the dark has a better chance of scoring than a shot untaken, and this might be the only shot I have at seeing Noah again for a very, very long time – you best believe I took it.

That's so cool! Well, if you'd like to meet up, I could stop by tomorrow afternoon or something?

Yeah I'd love to meet up! Tomorrow afternoon works fine. I'm staying like 5 minutes from the station, I'll come and find you there.

14

It's not just Noah, as it turns out. It's Noah and Griffin. They're both here, they both remember, my head just... can't handle it. By some pure, dumb luck, I have tomorrow afternoon off, on one of the only two days that Noah and Griffin are spending here. It's things like this make me wonder if it might be true that everything happens for a reason, as much as seventh grade me would've been absolutely cursing the idea.

My parents thought it was so cool that Noah was here, although they thought I was a bit silly for going all the way to Interlaken to meet him. Oh well, this is literally the only chance I'll have to meet up with him for a long time, I'm going to do it whether it's practical or not.

Sleep was the last thing on my mind that night. I knew I needed to, since I still had school in the morning, but the exitement was for the following afternoon was just unbearable. The idea alone of telling Sahil what I was going to do that afternoon had me grinning from ear to ear.

I didn't even need my alarm clock to wake up on time, which just happened to be an hour earlier than usual. Any other morning, I would've waited until the last possible second to crawl out of bed, but today, time can't march fast enough.

My clothes were already picked out and ready, I jumped out of bed and brushed my teeth, more awake than ever despite my lack of sleep. Mom and Dad had both already left for work by the time I'd gone down-stairs, so I had the house to myself to revel in my antic-ipation.

By the time Sahil got on the bus, I was practically bursting at the seams to tell him all about this afternoon. He waved to me from the doorway before sitting down next to me.

"He's here, Sahil, I can't believe it", I said, my voice impatient with excitement.

"The ticket collector?", Sahil asked, half asleep.

"No, *du Houz*, Noah."

"Woah, what? Are you serious?", he suddenly beamed to life.

"I'm serious! We're meeting up today."

"DUDE! That's crazy, I'm so happy for you! Is it just you and him?"

"Actually, he's with another old friend of ours, Griffin. He'll be there, too."

"I told you Noah didn't send a friend request just for the sake of it", Sahil said, a smug little smile on his face.

I couldn't concentrate at all through the morning. I spent all my time switching between the clock on my laptop and the clock in the classroom, hoping the hands would start moving just a little bit faster, but as time progressed, so did the size of the knot in my stomach.

By the time I was actually in the train, headed to our designated meet-up spot, my excitement had drained almost entirely in exchange for anxiety. It's been seven years... I don't even know these people. What do I talk about? How do I greet them? Do I just act like nothing's changed since we were ten?

Thoughts constantly flitted through my mind, most of them for no more than a second or two. I wondered if this was even a good idea in the first place... do I want this? What if this changes my whole perception of

Noah and Griffin, is it worth ruining the memories I have of home?

The train doors became more attractive with each passing station, but I stayed firm in my decision to stick it out, even if it felt like I was a nuclear reactor having a core meltdown on the inside. By the time I got to Interlaken my legs felt like pudding, I thought I might hurl waiting on the bench by the tourist office for Noah and Griffin.

"Cameron?", I heard a voice say from around the corner.

I couldn't help but smile when I saw the two of them. Noah really did look the exact same, just a bit bigger. He'd finally cut his cranial mop, although maybe just for this one occasion. Square jaw, big, buggy brown eyes, messy hair, a nose that's just a bit too big for his face. That's Noah. It took me a minute to register Griffin as Griffin. He was almost a whole head taller than

153

Noah, but the gibbon-like gangliness he suffered from as a kid had really evened itself out. His face was a lot more angular than I had remembered it, but he was also seven years older, so I'll give that a pass.

"Long time no see!", Noah exclaimed, pulling me into a hug.

I could barely even choke out the word "hello" I was so out of it. This is real life, for real. I'm here. They're here.

We're next to each other for the first time in seven years.

"How have you been, man?", Griffin asked, patting my back, the same way he'd patted it seven years ago.

"I've been good, wow. You look the same."

"So do you", Noah laughed.

"Is it alright with you if we quickly circle back to our hostel so the two of us can change real quick? It's like, five minutes from here, and then we'll walk down to the lake afterwards."

"We tried to do it yesterday, but we were so tired we gave up halfway through", Griffin said, smiling.

"Yeah absolutely, fine by me", I grinned.

I was expecting it to be a lot more… awkward. We walked a total of probably three hours, and the conversation flowed for all of it, really, as if I'd never left. It was unreal, I nearly forgot where I was.

For the first time in seven long years, I felt like I was home. And when we said our goodbyes after those three short hours, I felt like a little kid again, on the schoolyard, the last day of school, broken porcelain held together by Elmer's glue – only this time, I didn't have to pick up the pieces alone.

Fourth grade me would be cursing myself for saying this, so would fifth grade me, sixth grade me, seventh, eighth, ninth, and me like, four days ago, too; but dad was right. All along. Well, half-right.

I was a wreck the following day at school, but in the end, it was Sahil who helped me ride through each and every wave that came crashing down on me. It was Melina who reminded me that I wasn't alone in feeling like this, it was Amisa explained ways she always makes herself feel better she's homesick. It was Shahid who explained that homesickness comes in waves, and that I won't feel like this all the time. it was Mara who gave me the biggest hug she could possibly give, and it was Florian who told me the story of Odysseus and the way he longed for his day of return to help me think of other things.

Home isn't a place – it's a feeling. Home is security, home is familiarity, home is comfort. Home is the people you know you can fall back on if you need to, who always have your back, no matter what – home is wherever you decide to let yourself trust the people around you, wherever you feel like you belong, even if that means home is the most ragtag group of unlikely people who just happen to get each other.